the universe knows.

now go live your dream!

Thank you ☺

I really hope you enjoy the book...

Ron

manifested by
ron dinehart

the universe knows. now go live your dream!

Cover/Artwork design Michelle Valentino

Publisher's Cataloging-in-Publication data

Dinehart, Ron.
    The Universe knows : now go live your dream! / manifested by Ron Dinehart
    p. cm.
    ISBN 978-0-9903773-0-6 (pbk.)
    ISBN 978-0-9903773-1-3 (e-book)
1. Self-actualization (Psychology).
2. Self-realization. 3. Conduct of life.
4. Happiness. I. Title.

BF575.H27 D56 2014
158.1 --dc23   2014908476

visit us at:
www.theuniverseknows.com

the universe knows, inc.
publishing co.

This book is dedicated to all of the wonderful people who have supported me on my life's great journey.

Trish, my life partner, who has stood by me through all the ups and downs along this wonderful journey. Thank you, Trish, for everything you inspire me to become, for helping me stay grounded, and for teaching me what's really important in life.

My **mom,** who has inspired me in so many ways and always will.

Dad, the pragmatic voice and sage. Thank you, Dad, for being the perfect balance to my idealistic and spiritualistic mother.

Steve, one of my early angels who was there for me when I most needed support from the universe. From the bottom of my heart, I thank you for all you have done for me.

Carl, a trusted adviser and friend who is a terrific team player and always there when I need him.

Bernadette, for putting in countless hours in reviewing and editing major portions of this book.

To all the other wonderful angels that the universe provided to assist me along my journey - you know who you are!

~ welcome your angels. ~

gratitude changes everything.
~ the universe knows.

Foreword

Owning my own business was my dream. I didn't always know that. I wasn't listening.

That changed. I changed.

Today, I'm living my dream, and I'm the proud owner of one of the most awesome companies in the world: *the universe knows, inc.*

Yes, I'm proud and it's awesome. Why? Because the company's mission is to support the most important mission each of us has in our lifetime:

> *To live our unique purpose, follow our dreams, and never give up.*

To follow your dreams is to create a more rewarding life. It's not always easy.

Pursuing your dreams can be demanding. It requires courage, sacrifice, perseverance, a never-give-up attitude, and faith, the likes of which you may never have known before. Anything of greatness does not come easily, but keep this one thing in mind:

> *The universe rewards those who choose to follow their dreams.*

We all have the power to live our truths and follow our life purposes. As you embark on your journey, the challenges presented at first may intimidate you. Just keep in mind that the more you strive and push forward, the more your strengths are revealed and the easier it becomes.

There will be ups and downs along the way, but remember to trust the process. Realize that it is not necessarily the outcome that is important; rather, it is the journey.

Cherish the journey.

What follows is a compilation of unique *pearls of wisdom*. These pearls encourage strength and courage. They are designed to remind you of what you already know:

The infinite wisdom you brought into this world when you were born will lead you. Trust and let go. Breathe life in and enjoy the wonderful gift of life!

Reflect and meditate on each pearl. Cherish the pearls and call upon them during your journey. While they may seem to be simple statements, the *pearls of wisdom* are powerful tools that will empower you as you make your way through your life adventure.

I wish you the best of luck on your journey. I assure you each day is worth the effort.

Never give up.
Persevere.
Give more than you receive.
Don't take life too seriously.
Cherish the journey.

Remember: the universe knows.

Author's Story

Thank you for buying this book. I hope it helps you awaken to and live your passion! I cannot think of anything more important than doing what you were put here on earth to do. I am honored to be part of your journey.

This book was written many years ago, but somehow it just wasn't ready to be introduced to the world. Evidently, the release date of the book really wasn't up to me as much as it was the universe, which had its own timetable.

There are two lessons I learned from this experience, the first being to never give up on your dreams and to do what is required to make your dreams a reality. You must do the work; there is simply no way around this.

The second lesson is that the universe has its own agenda and timing for anything and everything that shows up (or not) in our lives. And it is when we are ready and have learned our lessons that these things (people, events, etc.) show up.

If this book had been published years ago as originally planned, I believe it would not have had the same impact as it will today.

Because I was much more reclusive back then, this book probably would be sitting all by its lonesome on some dusty shelf and its message and wisdom would have been lost. A new book needs its author to go out and speak publicly to promote its message - and back then I simply was not a willing and able participant.

So to overcome my shadows, I've made a conscious effort to get back into the world, face my insecurities, and connect again with people. The steps I've taken recently include joining my local chamber of commerce, joining a local Toastmasters club, making an effort to attend multiple business networking events every month, joining a small spiritual group that meets once every other month in someone's home, and even joining my local town's men's golf league (note: in the first tournament I played in, I won the president's cup - go figure).

This is all so important because I am facing my insecurities and shadows. And, as I have said, to properly promote the book (and company), I needed to get back into the public forum and get comfortable speaking in front of people to better convey the pearls within the book. In other words, I needed to walk the walk.

Everything is perfect - this I know. So thank you, universe, for your timing and for teaching me these valuable lessons.

With this I am going to trust the process and hope this book inspires you to take action in your life and to face your shadows head on - providing you with the courage to live your dreams - because life is way too short to do otherwise.

Shift your awareness, evolve and grow, and always remember to be in gratitude.

In the greater world, though, not much has changed since I first wrote this book. We are bombarded today by messages on how to dress, how to find the love of your life, what to eat, how to get your body in shape, how to make all the money in world...the list goes on and on. But you'll find, ironically, that when you start living your truth - your soul's journey - your awareness shifts. You notice the abundant miracles around you every day and just how precious life truly is. And your life is precious. You are precious.
Always remember this.

Your soul is your truth. It needs you to listen to its message and carry out its wish:

Live your life purpose.

Live the life your soul intended, and everything you dream of will follow. It is only when you discover what makes you happy and begin to live your soul's purpose that everything can start to fall into place. I am living proof of this.

I remember reading Death of a Salesman in college. What really stands out in my memory is the professor saying, "There is nothing more tragic in life than doing something for a living that you did not like." I smirked and thought, "How could anybody do something their whole life that they couldn't stand? That will never happen to me."

But something happened along the way.

After graduating from college, I entered the engineering field, embarking on a career path that I didn't really decide on, yet I chose. I know that sounds curious, but I guess I thought it was what I should do. I now realize that without awareness or understanding, I had been influenced by others' expectations and had begun robotically following traditional steps. I had yet to learn how much it would matter, but I was not living my purpose.

Life was normal, I guess. Work was work and I stayed the course. I met somebody and was married. We had two children (they are, by the way, my life angels; I know that one way the universe communicates to me is through them).

But something was not right. I became preoccupied with work and the corporate ladder. I did the dance but bristled at the strict, corporate way and the rigors of the engineering workday. My stress level and resentment grew. Increasingly, I was moody and depressed. I suppressed my feelings as best I could and continued to work under this cloud for thirteen years. One day, I couldn't bear it anymore. I crossed a threshold where my pain, numbness, and hopelessness were greater than my fear of failing.

I had to get away.

It was during a road trip, as I drove alone along a scenic stretch of highway through secluded farmlands, that a voice came to me. I was listening (for, perhaps, the first time). I suddenly knew what I was meant to do: live my dream and inspire others to live theirs.

The phrase "the universe knows" had been in my head for years. I knew it was a

powerful statement, and I liked it,
but I didn't know why. What happened to
me on that road trip was special. A
stream of honest, open, flowing thoughts
and realizations was released. I was
nourished by the thought of inspiring
others. There was no turning back. I
decided to follow my dream and start
my own business by making shirts with
"the universe knows" printed on them.

At first, I endured many questions and
some chuckles, but I never wavered. I
never questioned that voice. I acted
quickly without wondering about the
consequences and took my first step
toward living my dream. In August 2003,
the universe knows, inc. was born.

I now realize that in the thirteen years
leading up to that point, the universe
had been setting me up to live my soul's
purpose. I am grateful for my education as
well as the work experiences and
relationships that blossomed along the
way. I learned so much. I now know
that I had to go through it all - had to
experience enough to understand. I relate
to people with compassion and
understand what they are going
through because I went through it too.
It is only because I did it that I can
say it can be done.

We all have unique gifts, resources, and experiences. Our paths and dreams are different. Yet everyone's ability to live with purpose and passion is the same. Listen to your inner voice and trust that you have what it takes to live your dreams. Wherever you are in your life or on your life's journey, let the universe provide you with the encouragement you need to awaken your passion. Let it cheer you on to live your dreams. All you need to live your dream is an open heart and the willingness to learn what you already know.

Dare to dream.

Follow your heart.

The rewards are worth the risk.

This, the universe knows.

And my soul said
~ by ron dinehart

"Why didn't you take more chances in life?"

And I said "because I was afraid of failure
and rejection."

And the soul said "why didn't you stretch
your boundary more often?"

And I said "because I was comfortable
where I was."

And the soul said "why didn't you follow
your dreams and aspirations?"

And I said "because I felt I wasn't worthy."

And the soul said "Why didn't you love more
and be more vulnerable?"

And I said "because I was afraid of
getting hurt."

And the soul said "why didn't you embrace
life more and be more open to
the possibilities?"

And I said "because I was afraid of
the unknown."

And the soul said "why didn't you
love yourself?"

And I said "I am not really sure."

And the soul finally said in response that…

"Failure and rejection are necessities in life
that help you to grow and evolve as
a person.

And stretching your boundaries and
achieving great accomplishments are what
create joy and happiness in life.

You are so worthy of everything this life has
to offer. You are so worthy.

Realize that vulnerability is the key to loving
deeper. Vulnerability teaches you to trust
the process and have faith.

Learn that embracing the unknown is where
all the magic is.

And finally know you are loved so very
deeply. You always have been and always
will be, from now to eternity. And know
that I will never let you down."

And I said "thank you soul...I love you too."

And the soul said you're welcome...and know one thing - that it is never too late to live your dream...to live your purpose... never...now let's get started.

pearls of wisdom.

evolve and grow.

open yourself to possibility.

act on faith.

to act on faith is to live "on purpose."

when you follow your heart and pursue
your dream, the universe delivers
support and guidance.

in short the universe always has your
back and constantly provides you the
miracles to assist you in your journey.

the key is to stay open and notice
the messages.

to act on faith is to open yourself
to possibility.

follow the path of your purpose, and you
will know happiness each step of the way.

allow the miracle.

to allow the miracle is to believe in you.

everything you are stems from your
intentions and thoughts. the universe
echoes those thoughts and intentions and
delivers support for the direction you set.

if your thoughts are limiting and unsure,
uncertainty will grow. if you doubt yourself,
the universe will reflect that back to you,
reinforcing insecurity.

negative thoughts will not produce
positive results.

to allow the miracle, release pessimism,
and fill your mind and your heart with
confidence, breathe deeply and let go. to
allow the miracle, you must believe in
yourself. the universe will meet your
expectations, giving you exactly what
you think you are worthy of.

always look up.

"Life's greatest gifts often come wrapped in adversity." ~ Richard Paul Evans

life is not meant to be rosy all the time. what would be the point if it was? it is during the tough times and adversity where we learn to evolve and grow. adversity makes us stronger and helps us appreciate the good times even more.

when we always look up, we realize how grateful we are to be alive and how precious our life truly is. we say thank you more often and know that all will be well. always looking up builds our awareness and teaches us that the tough times we're going thorough won't last and that there is a brighter plan for you - even though you may not see it currently.

enjoy the ride and always look up.
the universe knows.

answer your calling.

to answer your calling is to live in sync
with your dreams.

to answer your calling, you must first
listen. what is your purpose? what makes
you you? what is the life you were meant
for? to answer your calling is to cherish
yourself and nourish your unique gifts,
setting the course for your life journey.

when you know your calling, the way to
answer it becomes clear. you gain courage,
knowing your course is the correct one and
the universe will support each step. your
world shifts and things fall into place.

happiness, joy, creativity, and passion
fill your cup. sounds good, right?

listen and you will know.

awaken your passion.

what delights you? what brings a smile
to your lips and a sparkle to your eye?
let more of that light into your life each
day and awaken your passion.

to awaken your passion is to ignite your
energy - to invigorate yourself with
whatever inspires you. is it hard to figure
out what your passion is? not really.

close your eyes and breathe deeply. think.
let your mind wander with just one goal
in mind: letting a smile come to your face.
when you realize the smile, simply notice
what it is that you are thinking of or
remembering. latch onto that thought
and let it swirl in your mind today.

tomorrow you'll know more. do it again. the
next day you'll know more. you will begin to
feel it. you are awakening your passion. you
will feel the energy. as you awaken
your passion, things will come to you.
explore, savor, follow your inspiration.

awaken your passion and let your joy grow.
your soul's energy will ignite and you will
simply glow.

summon the universe.

be bold enough.

be bold enough to allow great things
to happen.

to be bold enough is to have the courage to
let go of worries and insecurities. it is
to act on your own behalf in pursuit of
your dreams while simultaneously
putting forth grace and gratitude.

being bold is about having faith in the
universe. when we are bold, the magic
happens; we summon the universe to
send its angels and support us in our
greatest endeavors.

be bold enough for the universe to take
notice and reveal the power it intends
for you.

be here now.

be here now and enjoy this moment. this moment leads to the next. be there then.

every moment is what you make it. if you live in the past or the future, you miss out on what now is meant to be.

don't let it pass by unnoticed. the moment is a gift from the universe and that's why it's called the present.

be here now and know you are exactly where you are supposed to be. take your time; it belongs to you and has so much to give.

be in gratitude.

to be in gratitude is to appreciate
each moment and give thanks for all
we experience.

to be in gratitude is to thank the universe
each and every day for the beautiful gift of
life and every form it takes. whether for the
rustling sound of leaves when a breeze lifts
them, the sensation of strolling along
a sandy beach, or the power of your
beating heart, give thanks often.

to be in gratitude is to appreciate that
somebody loves you (probably more than
you even know).

when you are in gratitude, you will
remember to give thanks for simple things
such as laughter, as well as the friends,
family, or special person that you can
share that laughter with.

be in gratitude every day, and you will
have more to give thanks for.

be kind today.

one thing you always have at your disposal is kindness. being kind is realizing that we are all connected and that how you choose to treat others, as well as all living organisms on this planet, is ultimately a reflection of who you are.

and who you really are is...LOVE.

being kind could be as simple as offering a smile to someone, lending your ear, helping an elder across the street, or just saying thank you.

being kind is something that costs nothing and yet brings infinite abundance.

so be kind today, and every day, and watch your world blossom.

be the change.

Mohandas (Mahatma) K. Gandhi said, "We must be the change we wish to see in the world." this simple statement has enormous power.

in order to change the world, first we must change, and then we must shift our awareness. by listening to and observing our intentions and actions, we will see whether we are working effectively toward the world we want to create.

to be the change is to leave the world a better place for the future. it can only be so if each of us makes it so. it happens one by one and must continue day after day.

so start today. be the change and watch the world follow.

tap into your special gifts.

be the magic.

be the magic, and witness the changes
you wish for.

we are all born with our own unique gifts.
to be the magic, you simply need to tap
into your special gifts - to offer your talents
to the world and welcome what the universe
has in store for you.

the magic helps you step through fears and
challenges. it reinforces positive actions
and attitudes. what you put forth comes
back to you in multiples, so be the magic
and work wonders.

believe in yourself.

we all have what it takes to accomplish anything we set out to do, but we are often our own worst enemies. instead of taking action, we overanalyze and overthink. rather than "going for it," we judge ourselves too strongly, worry about too many things, and let life pass us by.

when we believe in ourselves, we can and do accomplish anything. we all have the strength, courage, and wisdom to achieve anything, but it is only when we take a chance that we prove this to ourselves.

your greatest accomplishments start with you. so decide what your next accomplishment will be. then, take a chance, work hard, and believe in yourself.

remember to be proud of yourself when you finish.

blessings are everywhere.

look around and take notice: the universe
is always talking to you, providing you
with clues to help you live your purpose.
are you listening?

blessings are everywhere, affirming that the
universe is always working for us and giving
us a strong foundation on which to grow.

listen.

you will learn what you need to know.

breathe in life.

live life with passion, live life to the fullest,
and cherish each moment. to breathe in
life is to live with gratitude and generosity
of spirit.

it is to embrace the unknown and challenge
ourselves to be our best. when we breathe
in life, we not only welcome all that is good
into our life but we also give of ourselves.

inhale...exhale...remember: we make
room to receive as much as we are willing
to give away.

celebrate little things.

little things make a big difference.

so often, we overlook little things that make our lives rich. we take simple things for granted and look to special events and occasions and the bigger things in life to make us happy. when you celebrate little things, you create happiness for yourself.

did you eat right and take care of yourself today? celebrate! did you wake rested and have the energy to accomplish what you needed to today? celebrate! you don't need to throw a party. there's no need to overindulge or spend anything to celebrate little things. simply recognize the positive of your day and smile. feel good about it. let that feeling grow.

celebrating little things increases the positive energy in and around you. celebrate little things, welcome the joy this process brings, and watch the little things grow.

cherish each fleeting moment.

cherish the journey.

how sweet it is: the journey of life.

to cherish the journey is, in a way, to cherish each fleeting moment as it passes by. it is to learn from the past, celebrate our history, and look forward to tomorrow.

to cherish the journey is to shift focus from the outcome, letting go enough to enjoy the process. when we cherish the journey, we know that we are exactly where we are supposed to be.

when you learn to cherish the journey, you will trust the process and be fueled by faith.

there may be bumps along the way, but the journey is what makes memories. cherish each one.

commit to yourself.

what comes first: family and friends? career? community? religion?

none of the above.

you are essential. in order to achieve anything - to be a good wife, husband, parent, or friend - you must make yourself a priority.

to commit to yourself is to agree to be the best you can be. it is to acknowledge your needs and nurture your soul. selfishness and greed do not play a role.

to commit to yourself, simply listen to your heart. remember that you are important and your thoughts, needs, emotions, and goals need as much time and care as others'.

commit to yourself. be as gentle and kind with yourself as you are with others. fuel and support your spirit and dreams. tend to your needs, and everything around you will blossom.

courage always wins.

this is a bold statement, but know that when you are bold, mighty forces will join you.

you were born with unique and genius talents that only you possess, and as the old adage goes, "Many are called yet few are chosen." answer your calling with courage.

the ones who are chosen are the dreamers who take action and have the courage to take on the responsibility that comes with fulfilling destiny.

courage always wins. always.

courage to risk.

"Jump and the net will appear." it's an old saying that holds truth when you are following your life purpose.

courage to risk can be tapped only when you truly believe in yourself.

in the pursuit of your dreams, you may find that you must take a leap of faith. this can be difficult, but when you are on the right course and in sync with your true purpose, what might have seemed a leap before becomes just a step.

the universe reaches up to you when you reach out to it.

create your legacy.

a life lived with adventure, integrity, love, compassion, and joy is a life well lived.

pursue your passions with all your heart, connect with others along the way, and create your legacy without even trying.

live with intention and gratitude, and your legacy will deliver extraordinary gifts for generations to come.

it's all about perspective.

do something awesome.

small or big, awesomeness is just that: awesome.

awesome changes the world.

this pearl is intentionally vague because one person's awesome may be entirely different than another's.

it's all about perspective.

but one thing we can all agree on is that doing something awesome changes the world; so do something awesome so when you look back on your life, you will smile and be at peace.

embrace the moment.

to embrace the moment is to realize how
precious life is and that each day is a gift.
when you embrace each moment, you
agree to live in the "now," taking in all
that surrounds you.

it is about awareness.

there is a certain calm you will know when
you embrace the moment.

when you embrace the moment, you quickly
build a new habit. it becomes easier to trust
the process and be in gratitude.

ultimately you realize the moment is
all we have.

slow down just a bit. breathe life in
and embrace the moment.

it is addicting.

evolve and grow.

life is about growing, learning, and evolving. it is about becoming a better person each day, doing something that fulfills you.

your soul chose this life to grow and expand through life's many experiences.

forgive yourself for past mistakes, love yourself, and move forward. make each tomorrow better than today. what does that take? just be: observe, listen, learn.

your attitude and energy will change.

it's almost effortless. let it happen.

expect the best.

attitude is everything. it's also a choice.

Einstein once said that the single most important decision we will make in our lifetime is whether the universe is friendly or not.

when you expect the best, you've made that important decision and you know the universe is on your side. expect the best, and that is what you will experience.

some choices are difficult. this is not one of them.

face the obstacles.

life is full of obstacles. how we deal with
them is what determines success.

we all face challenges in life. to face the
obstacles is to view your challenges as
lessons. these lessons can represent
opportunities - the chance to grow, learn,
or adjust.

obstacles may also be clues or reminders.
when you encounter an obstacle, know it
is there for a reason. do you need to slow
down and focus? have your priorities gotten
mixed up? or have you perhaps forgotten
an important pearl?

the universe strides alongside us
throughout our journey. it
communicates with us. listen.

face the obstacles, and as you meet them,
contemplate the potential purpose or
message. put the lessons the universe
gives you to good use.

see what's most important.

find your balance.

life is hectic. we could all use a little balance in our lives. balance is steady, strong, and easy.

to find your balance is to prioritize.

put what is important ahead of everything else and the tables shift. your perspective changes, and it becomes easier to see what is most important. it then becomes even easier to keep the important things in the forefront; and suddenly, we are spending the majority of our energy on those things that matter most to us. our health, our families, and our friends get the attention they deserve. we rush a little less and spend a little more time with things that fulfill us.

focus and faith.

anything is possible.

when living your truth and pursuing your dream, you will be empowered by focus and faith. cultivate this remarkable combination and harness the power of your innermost strength.

"the bonk" is a term in endurance sports. bonking is a condition that occurs when glycogen levels are depleted. when athletes bonk, they need carbohydrate-rich food or drink to restore their energy and strength. when you feel depleted, focus and faith are the fuel you need to fortify you along your adventure.

focus and faith will enable you when you think you have no more to give. they are the power behind fortitude, and they deliver wisdom when it's needed most.

focus your intentions.

if one day you want blue and the next
day you want red, the universe may
give you purple.

mixed messages and confusion can
create chaos and more confusion. a direct
approach works best. to have a satisfying
journey toward your dream, focus
your intentions.

when you are consistent in thought and
action, you will be inspired by the steady
progress you make. you will experience less
frustration and disappointment, fewer
distractions, and more joy along the way.

take the time you need to figure out your
passion and purpose. be clear about what
you intend, and commit to yourself.

the shortest distance between two points
is a straight line.

follow your heart.

follow your heart, and you will never be let down. the reason you are here is in your heart. it is your soul - your purpose. when you follow your heart, you are living your truth and the universe will reward you.

the easy route is, well, easier. many of us take the easy route not for fear of hard work but for fear of failure. don't be afraid of either. to live a more fulfilling life, follow your heart.

those who "have heart" wow us all. they impress us with their accomplishments. we admire them because they are remarkable. but guess what: we all have heart. remarkable people simply follow theirs.

free your spirit.

freedom. it's one of the most universally valued states of being. wars have been fought to win it and holidays created to celebrate it.

we all want to be free. your spirit needs to be free. listen for your inner voice. if you hear nothing, it's telling you something important. before anything else, you must free your spirit. remove judgment and self-doubt. release worry and anger. relieve tension and negativity. your spirit will stretch. you will feel the process.

listen again for your inner voice. you may hear it right away. it may take some time.

when you've freed your spirit, you will know. you will be in tune with your heart's vision, and you will hear your inner voice. you will feel the power of your unique gifts and you will know how to nourish your newly freed spirit.

you will be liberated, and you will celebrate.

honor your soul.

gather your courage.

the cowardly lion always had courage.
he just didn't know it.

gather your courage and let doubt
disintegrate. you have within you exactly
what you need to accomplish your dreams.
doubt and fear hold us back.

courage moves us forward.

doubt and fear are learned. courage
is innate.

to gather your courage, honor your soul
and have faith in the universe. trust that
you can accomplish everything you set your
mind to. believe that the universe will not
give you something you can't handle.

you were born with courage. you don't need
a wizard to help you find it.

get excited again.

Rome wasn't built in a day. but however long it took, i bet they were pretty darn excited about it along the way.

you are making changes for the better. no, scratch that. you are making changes for the best. get excited again! change doesn't happen overnight.

the process is exhilarating.

the progress is thrilling. every day, as you work toward your dreams, you have reason to get excited again.

reinvigorating yourself with purpose and direction, setting goals and striving to reach them - these are exciting activities. you are enriching your life experience and affecting those around you.

as you progress, you will inspire others. as you grow, you will experience more joy. as you rewrite your script, you will create opportunities and experience great things.

there's not a travel brochure in the world that offers anything as exciting as what's in store for you. read the previous paragraph and get excited again.

give of yourself.

we are all in this together.

giving is an investment. when you invest
in something, you believe it will grow
and deliver positive returns.

when you give of yourself, you are investing
in the goodwill of others and the generosity
of the universe.

to give of yourself is to help those in need.
it is to be generous with kindness. give of
yourself by offering encouragement and
support to those on their life's journey.

when it comes to making this world a better
place, the more we give, the more we get.

give yourself hugs.

giving yourself hugs is about accepting
and loving yourself. It is appreciating our
"humanness" and realizing that we are not
perfect and that it is OK to make mistakes.

when we give ourselves hugs, we
acknowledge these imperfections and
actually embrace them inside of us.

by loving ourselves first, we become able
to love others. so give yourself that big hug
each day and watch your world change...
you are beautiful...the universe knows.

hold your vision.

they say hindsight is twenty-twenty. i say hold your vision, and you will see more clearly and with more certainty.

to hold your vision is to stay true to your values. remain steady and focused with a clear perspective on what matters to you.

when you hold your vision, others' expectations blur and have less impact on your decisions. you're able to stay true to yourself, confidently.

be clear about who you are and what you stand for, and then hold strong and steadfast. maintain your stance. be consistent, and your fortitude strengthens.

when you stand strong and firm, the universe provides a foundation to match. hold your vision, stand tall, and look about. you'll enjoy the scenery.

i am enough.

just for today.

what a difference a day makes.

just for today, i am going to allow myself to be imperfect. i will forget my past and not worry about the future.

today, i will love myself, forgive myself, and relinquish any feelings of guilt that i have.

just for today, i will accept that i am sacred. today, i will know that i am enough. just for today, i will stretch my boundaries and push just beyond my comfort zone.

today, i will smile more and be more generous. just for today, i will be grateful for the simple things, celebrate little things, and allow myself to be loved.

today will be a good day and tomorrow, when it arrives, will become today.

keep hope alive.

especially in these tough and challenging times, it is essential that we keep our hope alive. it is in these darkest moments - just when we are about to give up - that the miracle will happen.

this is the universe's way of seeing how bad we really want something.

keeping hope alive is knowing that the universe is always right here, rooting for us and concerting its blessings for us.

the key is to never ever give up and always keep alive your hope that the miracle will happen...and it will...always...the universe knows.

know in stillness.

each year, trees know when the time
comes to blossom.

inside each of us is infinite wisdom. when
we are still and peaceful, we tap into the
abundant source of our creation.

to know in stillness is to center our souls
and quiet our minds. it is to let awareness
grow and to renew the sense of self
and purpose.

know in stillness and connect to the
universe. set aside time from your day,
settle your spirit, and know that in
stillness you will find the focus, clarity,
and wisdom to grow and become
your full self.

lead by example.

inspired people inspire people.

positive energy is powerfully influential.
when you are on your life's path, following
your soul's direction, you are light, joyful,
and magnetic.

you attract positive energy because you
are positive energy.

you are fueled from internal resources
and you ignite external sources. we are all
mirrors to those around us, and those
around us reflect the energy they see in us.

lead by example. let others see who you
really are - a truly magnificent being,
capable of anything you set your mind to.
smile broadly and let your energy shine.
you will inspire all around you to strive
for that glow.

live your life purpose and others will
follow. their mirrors will reflect brightly
back to you.

learn to laugh.

let that gentle smile grow.

feels good, right?

impish, broad, toothy - whatever your smile is, bring it on. you will immediately feel uplifted.

giggle.

you are in charge. you can choose how to feel. you can also choose how to react.

humor is your natural state and also a wonderful gift. use it. learn to laugh, and you change your world.

listen to a child's laugh, and you are hearing the joy of life. that joy is yours to connect with. it is your choice to accept the joy in your life. we forget sometimes that life is spontaneous. we take ourselves too seriously. we laugh too little and think too much.

accept your imperfections. life is funny. learn to laugh and nurture your soul.

let life excite you.

let abundance flow.

loosen your grip.

abundance is yours. it is everywhere. to let abundance flow is to live your life with hopeful expectation. you cannot know what tomorrow will bring, and that is exciting. you wake and have a whole day to make a difference. that is exciting.

each day is filled with opportunity.

greet each day with expectation.

let life excite you.

you have the wheel. steer your course, relax your grip, look ahead, and let abundance flow.

live for today.

each day is your day.

live for today because it is all yours. no matter what the day has in store for you, embrace it. if you can make it memorable, do so. you are here. you have the day. it may not be perfect, but it is life.

live for today and appreciate all that you are and all that you aspire to be. acknowledge the good. accept the bad.

life is a gift. unwrap each day with enthusiasm and your gifts will keep giving.

live in abundance.

when we live in abundance, we
acknowledge the infinite source of potential
and supply that the universe has ready
and available to us all.

we know that whatever we give away will be
given right back to us tenfold because there
is infinite supply.

we realize that there is plenty of
everything to go around for everyone and
that if one person wins, another must
win as well - there are no losers.

when we live in abundance, we realize that
whatever we choose to manifest and realize
will be given to us. so dream bigger than big
and shift your awareness - you are worthy -
the universe knows.

live in wellness.

we make choices every day that affect the rest of our lives.

positive thoughts are key to positive health. choose to live in wellness, and choices become easier.

connect with your soul and it will guide you.

think positive. be positive. your body is a miracle and you decide where it takes you.

live in wellness and enjoy well-being. make choices that serve the miracle of you.

our natural state is healthy and pure.
live in wellness and let your body - let the miracle - thrive.

live with passion.

to live with passion is to continually stretch your boundaries, extending beyond what you thought possible. it is the willingness to leave your safe harbor and venture out to unknown, uncharted territory. to live with passion is to realize that it is in not knowing that you will find magic.

living with passion is the ultimate in living your purpose. when you live with passion, you live from the heart instead of from the mind.

you make the rules of your life instead of your life making the rules for you.

dare to be different and live creatively, and doors will open.

your intentions and your thoughts shape your life. follow your heart, have faith, live with passion, and let your life take whatever shape you choose.

experience life.

live your truth.

the truth will set you free.

step out from behind the walls you've
built and the masks you wear, and
experience life.

live your truth, and life rewards you.
material possessions do not define you.
expectations do not define you.

your spirit defines you. you must listen to
it. to feel satisfied and live fulfilled,
you must live your truth.

if we are always performing for others,
life is only a stage. live your truth and
become a star.

love without limits.

nobody is perfect.

love without limits and accept others for who they are. it's a give-and-take situation. when you love without limits, you will be loved without limits. you will be accepted for who you are.

that bears repeating: you will be accepted for who you are. that feels pretty good.

what goes around comes around. cliché? maybe. nevertheless, it is true. love without limits, and let yourself be loved. we are all in this together, and the more you give, the more you get.

cliché? maybe.

or maybe just a universal truth.

make a difference.

making a difference is about one thing:
living your unique life purpose.

when you are living your life purpose, you
are, by default, making a difference. the
courage to follow your dreams and live
your truth is powerful and contagious.

the changes in you will inspire those
around you and encourage them to
follow their hearts.

to make a difference, you need to live
with passion, believe in yourself, and be
positive. the influence you will have on
those around you will start a chain
reaction. more dreams will awaken, more
people will find their purpose, and more
people will make a difference.

and your influence will continue to grow.

notice the messages.

beep. bing. ding. ring. you have mail.
your chat is on. instant message
notification sent.

the messages you expect alert you. you
can't miss them.

yet the messages we don't expect are the
important ones. there are no notifications,
no alerts. adjust your focus and you will
notice the messages. extract yourself from
the noise of the day. log off, pick your head
up, and look around. the universe is
guiding us each day.

pay attention.

next time a stranger reaches out to help
you or you hear that song that brings a
fond memory back, receive the message.
take heed of what the universe is trying to
convey. clues, reminders, encouragement,
spirit lifters...the universe created
instant messaging.

we just have to notice the messages.

open all possibilities.

the shortest distance between two points
is a straight line.

a straight line may be the shortest distance,
but unless you travel "as the crow flies," the
straight line may not be the best course to
get from here to there.

open all possibilities and let the universe
show you the right way. focus on the
"what," not the "how," and experience all
that you are intended to live along the way.

free the reins, loosen your grip, and let
the universe guide you. when you open all
possibilities, you invite life to come to you.
allow the journey to be scenic, direct, fast,
slow. it will be more than you expected.

trust in your world. travel light. open all
possibilities, and arrive in style!

you are the artist.

paint your canvas.

your life is your masterpiece. you are born with a blank canvas and a toolbox of colors and textures. you are the artist. paint your canvas with every brush and stroke, as well as with every color.

everything in your life is a result of choices made. you can always paint over what you've already painted.

it's your life. make it beautiful.

paint your rainbow.

when a rainbow appears, we are naturally compelled to stop and admire it. rainbows have a special place in history, literature, and music. they are rare things of beauty that capture our attention and touch our souls. the beauty of a rainbow is simple and pure.

at our deepest core is our truest, most beautiful self. we are simple and pure in our essence, and when we paint our rainbow, we let that beauty shine through. paint your rainbow and let your true colors show.

celebrate all that you are and the special gifts inside. let all your colors shine through and release the beauty of your soul. those around you will be compelled to stop and admire.

play your symphony.

there is no end to the number of
combinations that can be made to
create music.

the options are limitless. and so it is
with your life. you are the composer. you
play the instruments. you create the
melodies - the tempo, rich sounds,
dramatic crescendos, and refrains.

play your symphony and hear
your creativity.

listen to your soul's sound and masterful
composition. we are composers of our own
lives. play your symphony and add to it.
build on it. make it loud, smooth, upbeat,
melodious. the options are limitless.
play it your way and make it memorable.

quiet your mind.

a state of inner peace and contentment.
that phrase alone inspires. we all crave
a peaceful state.

quiet your mind and let serenity guide you.
gain clarity. find out who you really are and
what inspires you.

it is not always easy. sometimes a quiet
mind seems so far away. make time to
find it. work for it. thoughts will pop into
your mind. let them float away.
keep trying. breathe.

when you quiet your mind once, it becomes
a little easier the next time. you will find
solace. it is worth the effort.

stay with your inner being and let the world
and all your worries wander away. quiet
your mind and enjoy a sense of peace.

quiet your mind, accept your peace, and
energize your spirit. when you quiet your
mind, you can listen to your soul and see
things with more clarity and focus.

rewrite your script.

many of us allow past experiences to define our future. while it is important to learn from the past, it is equally important not to live in it.

let go of negative self-perceptions and the expectations of others.

rewrite your script by freeing your mind of worries and "what ifs." redefine your beliefs about yourself, lift limitations, and step out of your comfort zone.

your life starts now. let go of past patterns and create the life you always wanted. live your way, looking forward, and the universe will reward you.

search for your truth.

seek your summit.

when we seek our summit, we search for
our truth and our highest self.

when we search for our truth, we
ultimately find our inner peace. and when
we find our inner peace, we find joy.

reach tall, climb high, and search
for knowledge.

seek your summit and discover your
life's adventure.

set into motion.

change requires action.

whatever you want to do, you can. you must simply decide what it is and then set into motion the "ingredients," or factors, that will help you get there.

setting into motion is taking the first step toward manifesting your dreams into reality. focus and faith are keys to success when you set into motion.

be very clear what it is you intend to manifest, set it into motion, and stay focused on the outcome.

it is up to you to set into motion; the universe will help keep your momentum.

shift your awareness.

"We do not see things as they are, we see them as we are." ~ Anaïs Nin

change your perspective, and you change your world.

when we shift our awareness and start to see things with a refreshed perspective, we start to notice more.

shift your awareness and gain new appreciation for the simple things around you. awaken your senses and refresh your spirit by simply seeing things with new, more positive energy.

shift your awareness, and you might also become more in tune with your own presence. when you start to see things around you differently, you also change. clarity, gratefulness, and patience come to you.

you see your own role differently. you understand your responsibility for your destiny and begin to understand that you own your destiny.

shift your awareness, change your perspective, and watch your life change.

soon is now.

"Life moves pretty fast. if you don't stop and look around once in a while, you could miss it." ~ Ferris Bueller

life is precious and will move by you in the blink of an eye if you don't stop and smell the roses.

the only way to slow down your life is to constantly stretch your boundaries and seek new experiences.

live in each and every moment with love, courage, and gratitude.

start today, with your feet firmly planted on the ground so that you bloom where you are currently planted.

sprinkle your joy.

happiness begets happiness. sprinkle your joy and set off a chain reaction.

young children smile a lot. they spread their joy and make us smile. they seem to innately understand that when you smile, the world smiles back at you.

so first test it out: smile when you feel down. yes, force it. feel the energy. with that little bit of effort, you'll realize, remarkably, you feel less somber.

now, have some fun with this: smile at a coworker, at a neighbor. catch people off guard as you spread your joy, and enjoy the reaction. you'll feel more joy and gain fuel to spread your joy. it's fascinating and life changing.

it is one of the most powerful tools in our tool set. sprinkle your joy, and it comes back to you tenfold.

the path becomes clear.

stand in integrity.

when no one is looking, do you do the right thing? the universe always knows.

integrity is your internal compass - your own north star. to get where you want to be, stand in integrity, and the path becomes clear.

our integrity guides us to become who we are meant to be. when we stand in integrity, we honor ourselves as well as those around us. we are empowered because our consciences are clear. our "accounts" with the universe are paid in full.

stand in integrity, and reap the rewards.

stir your soul.

stir a pot of soup on the stove and watch
all the ingredients line up in unison and
swirl smoothly in the pot. carrots, potatoes,
noodles - whatever you have in that soup
will almost dance. change direction. no
problem. all the ingredients pull an
about-face and dance the other way.
make crazy eights with the spoon.
watch the soup have fun.

stir your soul and get all your "life
ingredients" dancing. you can align your
ingredients in the direction you choose.
when you stir your soul, you awaken your
potential, because you command your
energies and life forces to work together.

working in specific direction? good for you.
stir your soul and advance quickly. not
quite sure what direction you're heading in?
that's OK. stir your soul in some way - any
way - and awaken your passions; let your
life ingredients show you the way.

stretch your boundary.

what is your safety zone? do you wish it were different? stretch your boundary. challenge yourself to do something that feels bigger each day.

your life grows or shrinks proportionately to the fears you face head on.

to stretch your boundary is to mix things up just enough to energize your spirit and teach yourself that sometimes doing the things that make you just a bit uneasy makes you feel a bit more alive.

when you stretch your boundary, you increase your joy. you grow stronger and start to push through the limitations you've assigned yourself.

stretch your boundary and expand your world.

take the time.

stop reading this.

that's right. put the book down and
look around.

breathe. relax. think.

breathe. relax. breathe more deeply.

take the time to appreciate what you have,
or decide what you want to change.

take the time you need to live in
the moment.

take the time you need to nurture yourself.

take the time to feel the life you are
blessed with.

trust the process.

to trust the process is to trust that you are exactly where you are supposed to be.

many of us are planners. we want things to happen according to a schedule. sometimes we expect things to happen because "it's about time" or because we think we're ready. the timing for our lives, however, is not up to us.

to trust the process is to acknowledge that the universe will bring whatever it is we deserve or need when the time is right. have focus and faith. trust and let go. the future does not happen on our clocks or on our calls.

trust the process, have patience, smile, and enjoy each moment, because it's worth the wait and it may be here before you know it.

trust yourself.

trust your wisdom.

a gut feeling. instinct. drive and determination. trust your wisdom to navigate you to your destiny.

always listen to yourself. it is important to trust yourself. trust your soul and trust your wisdom. your first instinct is your best choice.

so often, we wait and let outside forces make decisions for us. we hesitate and delay. we take the safe route, perhaps because we fear failing but probably because we do not trust our own guidance systems.

when in doubt, trust your wisdom. and then just smile when you want to tell everyone you were right.

uphold your values.

our values are our internal moral
compasses. when we honor our values
and stand up for what we believe in, we
move mountains.

we are not here on this planet to simply go
through the motions and let life take us
aimlessly in any direction it chooses. we are
creators of our own destinies. we are here to
follow our passions and live our purposes.

when we uphold our values, we stand up
for what we believe in. the great Martin
Luther King Jr. said, "If we don't stand for
something, we fall for anything" - so i ask
you: what do you stand for?

always let your internal value system guide
you, and use it along your journey - you
will create magnificent things in your life
when you uphold your values.

visualize the outcome.

athletes use a mental technique to improve performance. they picture themselves crossing the finish line, winning the game, getting the perfect score. they visualize the outcome to imprint it and manifest it.

visualize the outcome you want and improve your performance. you will create and attract what you believe and intend.

visualize the outcome, and you will see the strength of your spirit and the power of the universe come together to propel you forward.

walk with confidence.

half of doing anything is believing
that you can.

you are your greatest resource, and it is
important to stand tall and be confident
in your actions. when you walk with
confidence, not only do you feel better
about yourself but the universe stands in
support of you. walk with confidence, and
doors open that were seemingly never
there before.

to walk with confidence, we must often
start with baby steps because cultivating
esteem and belief in yourself takes time.
but remember with each step, you are on
your way. believe in yourself, and keep in
mind life is a marathon, not a sprint.
you will get there.

we're all connected.

we all share the same planet and one universe. everything in the universe is one, and what you do unto the universe ultimately affects what the universe bestows on you.

every intention and action you set forth creates a wave of energy. that energy becomes universal. it changes forms but never dissipates. it will come back to you in one way or another.

let that concept weigh into everything you do, and remind others that what they do matters too. send out what you want to receive, and because we're all connected, you'll start to understand that the way you treat others and the world around you is really how you treat yourself.

what goes around really does come around.

cherish the unknown.

welcome new beginnings.

if you always knew the ending, would you ever read books (or watch movies)?

we don't need to know what lies ahead.

welcome new beginnings and grow from each and every experience.

let change come to you.

new beginnings mean you are on your way. welcome them and celebrate the newness of another chapter in your life book. turn the pages with enthusiasm.

cherish the unknown. it is where all the magic is.

you may not know where a new road will lead you, but have faith that it is a road meant for you.

life is an adventure. it is not knowing that makes it all so special.

welcome new beginnings and live a "best-seller" life.

welcome your angels.

a wise friend once told me that certain
people come into your life for a reason.
they may not stay long, but they will make
a difference that you will not forget.

they are your angels.

angels walk among us and have a purpose.

welcome your angels and allow their
blessings. allow their messages and
guidance to support your well-being. you
may not realize it as it is happening, but
your angels will deliver what you need
when you need it.

remember: they may not stay long, so
welcome your angels; cherish the time you
have, let go when you need to, and look
back fondly when you realize all they
did for you.

why wait? create.

a very large sneaker company has
inspired millions with its worldwide
campaign: just do it.

it's a message that is so simple yet
so powerful.

the company's marketing message speaks
to athletes at every level.

"why wait? create" speaks to everybody
on this planet. what do you admire? what
do you want to do? don't just stand
there - do it! why wait? create.

your masterpiece awaits.

get started.

do something different today. be curious.
ask questions. figure out what your
colors are.

your masterpiece awaits. it's just a matter
of deciding to let it flow. pay attention to
yourself today. let your soul breathe. you
are a creator. what will you do with that
gift? create friendships. create peace.
create comfort. create joy.

make your life a masterpiece of all that
you are capable of.

your treasure's within.

search your soul.

believe in yourself.

walk with confidence.

all we need is right inside of us. that's where your treasure is. right inside.

About the author

Ron Dinehart is the chief executive messenger of the universe knows®, inc., a global apparel and gift company that promotes positive living through its line of high-energy inspiration wear® apparel, gifts, and accessories.

Its mission is to be a model change agent for the world, awakening the wisdom within and dedicated to inspiring everyone to live their dreams with passion, purpose, and courage. It instills this through its innovative spirit and commitment to integrity.

Ron currently resides in Glen Cove, New York, with his longtime girlfriend, Trisha, and their beagle, Winnie. Ron has two beautiful children, Jordan and Paige. Ron is an avid music lover as well as a golf fanatic - both as a player and fan.

Please visit www.theuniverseknows.com to learn more about Ron and the universe knows, inc., products.

Made in the USA
Charleston, SC
13 July 2014